The Little Book of
Joe's Sh!t Life

By Kevin Hare

Contents

SAME OLD SH!T	1
CROCK OF SH!T	13
SCARED AS SH!T	28
TAKE A SH!T	37
DEEP SH!T	52
GIVE A SH!T	62
HOLY SH!T	70
NO SH!T	79
I SH!T YOU NOT	86
SH!TS & GIGGLES	93
MORE	97

Dedication

This book is dedicated to anybody out there who feels the world doesn't make any sense.

© 2016 Kevin G Hare

All rights reserved. No part of this publication may be reproduced, distributed, or transmitted in any form or by any means, including photocopying, recording, or other electronic or mechanical methods, without the prior written permission of the publisher, except in the case of brief quotations embodied in critical reviews and certain other noncommercial uses permitted by copyright law.

Same Old Sh!t

Let's meet Joe. Joe lives a good life. He has a good job that provides a good income which he uses to pay his mortgage, loan, credit cards and taxes. His job gives him three weeks vacation every year and he always makes sure his passport is good, he always carries his driver's license and has never even had a speeding ticket or been audited because he does everything by the book.

His average working day begins with a shower, a quick breakfast and coffee while catching what he can of the morning news. While he eats he has his phone in front of him browsing Facebook statuses that make him chuckle, he'll like a post with an inspirational quote or sometimes he reads something that he finds so profoundly stupid so he comments to the writer of the post that he's being an idiot and should research his facts better. He can't stand people who post that crap. When it's time, he begrudgingly repeats his regular commute to work, stopping at the convenient store quick to get his lottery tickets before showing up ten minutes early as he always does. He has a coffee mug in his lunch kit he got for Christmas one year that reads 'Head down & ass up' with a cartoon picture of a guy buried in paperwork at his desk.

He has a coworker, Bill, who works the same shift. Joe hates Bill. Bill is a bit arrogant and everyone knows it but he likes to seek Joe out every day just to find something to tease him about. One day it may be Joe's shirt, a movie he hasn't watched yet, a sticker of Yoda he has on his thermos, or his coffee mug because Bill has an endless repertoire of butt crack jokes. Joe's shoulders slump every time he hears Bill's voice entering into the meeting shack on the job site as he makes his morning rounds of greeting everybody with his boisterous tone. He has wondered why management hasn't confronted Bill about it but everyone seems to laugh at his antics so maybe no harm, no foul. Joe has wanted to go in several times but maybe management would think him a troublemaker, a guy who stirs the pot and he can't afford to lose his job. So Joe endures.

At the end of his 12-14 hour day he gets to go home, relieved that another day is over and find himself some dinner. He eats that in his favourite chair and tunes in to the daily news to see what's happening in the world. He is interested in seeing how the government's latest economic decisions are going to affect his life. His chosen industry is looking bleak and cutbacks have already begun. It upsets him that the official he elected got in and his actions since he won seem to be going against what's best for the people. Guess Joe will have to change his vote next time. After that, he might find a rerun of Cops or maybe a reality show he can laugh at. Those people are crazy, why would anyone willingly go on television and prove how dumb they are? Not Joe, he'll never do something like that. When he's tired, he goes to bed and tomorrow he will repeat the entire process.

Joe needs to grow up.

That is not necessarily mean to state Joe is an immature, whiny-baby-poo-poo-pants but if he could step outside of himself for just a minute, he needs to take an objective look at his life and how he reacts to it. What does he post or blog about - personal thoughts and feelings about how great the world is or how stupid some complete stranger may be for expressing an opinion no matter the level of education that prompted it?

He knows he doesn't want to be like Bill who resorts to the pain of others to feel better. Joe just watches tv and gets caught up in the bad stuff and other people's dirty laundry he forgets how he is supposed to live. Well, except at Christmas time when everybody is still trying to figure out the meaning of it all. He has always noticed how almost every seasonal show created is about finding the true meaning of Christmas. It incites laughter. Does mankind not get it yet? Ah wait, how can that happen if phrases like 'Merry Christmas' are banned and not allowed anymore because the goody goody feelings of togetherness and good will towards all may offend somebody. No wonder why the new generation is oblivious to old concepts like friendship, unity, loyalty or patriotism.

Joe may find it easier to react within the safe boundaries of social media without adding a 'true' voice behind it. Most can't drudge up enough concern to be bothered to do that. They aren't taught to fear consequence for what Joe thinks others are thinking of him matters more, especially if he thinks in a non-conforming manner. Golly, someone may think he is stupid for expressing an opinion without understanding the level of education that may have prompted it.

This is the society Joe lives in. This is his reality. Think he knows anyone who remembers a time before cell phones and internet? Communication was done on a personal level not a digital one. Kids went outside and 'played'. They got cuts, sprains and breaks, they got stung and bit without going into a coma. They stuck their tongues to frozen metal posts and got stronger and wiser for it. A single generation later, kids are home schooled and interact socially via texting. The generation after them will be short-armed, squinty-eyed, near-sighted, droopy-headed weaklings who won't have a clue what another human being looks like because they will only focus on themselves and their phones. This generation is already forgetting how to be personal. That's scary! These people are to be the next leaders, teachers or scarier yet, innovative thinkers. The problem is the system is not teaching them how to think, the system is teaching them how to obey.

To say that social media should be banned because it's bad for us is not the mission. People learn from bad things. People learn right from wrong, good from evil, gain perception and insight on how to do better. That is the balance upon which the world is maintained. No one can fully understand any single thing without observing its opposing force. Take verse 2 of the Tao Te Ching:

When people see some things as beautiful,

other things become ugly.
When people see some things as good,
other things become bad.

Being and non-being create each other.
Difficult and easy support each other.
Long and short define each other.
High and low depend on each other.
Before and after follow each other.

Therefore the Master
acts without doing anything
and teaches without saying anything.
Things arise and she lets them come;
things disappear and she lets them go.
She has but doesn't possess,
acts but doesn't expect.
When her work is done, she forgets it.
That is why it lasts forever.
      From a translation by S. Mitchell

This verse is just pointing out that opposites are part of the harmony that is life. The contrast of all things lives within Joe and he does not need to control them, only accept them for what they are. Do not focus on the labels of pretty and ugly, good and bad, things are what they are.

Reviewing man's history should have, by now,

taught him how to do better. How long have wars been waged on himself, harmed himself, hated, ridiculed and controlled himself? How long does it take to truly come to understand himself, to know how to truly benefit from making things better for someone else? There's a term for that - altruism. Who is up on history enough to know if a society ever got it right? Has not every culture in every age been founded and maintained on the exact same methods? A governing body or ruler (higher beings) making the decisions that apply to everyone else (lesser beings) under the guise that it is for their better interests because said lesser beings have not the capacity to do for themselves? That was the way it was done in ancient tribal clans, and that seems to be the way it is still done today.

Wars have always been based on territory, belief, politics and, hopefully Joe guessed it, pride and patriotism. Only these days there's an added element that has outclassed all other reasons - cash flow. There is profit to be made from warring and killing now. Sad it is to think how little value is put into life over 'legal tender'. How an individual life is so easily classified as collateral damage to steer an economy.

If you are unaware, our current currency is labelled a fiat monetary system. There has been no intrinsic value in 'money' since 1933, that's why 'this note is legal tender' is printed on bills and not 'this is actual money'. Any note has a nomination decreed to it by the government and can be traded for goods for that amount. That means, that note or 'promissory note' is a promise to pay and is of no use to the receiver until he trades it off or deposits it into an account to show as an asset to him.

Over the course of a lifetime, everyone is submitted to the same hints, the same signs that are literally screaming to change perceptions. Social media has actually helped to exemplify this idea.

Over and over Joe witnesses posts about the effects of destruction, the power of healing, the benefits good will makes on others and to himself, the stuff that creates the joy-joy feelings that make him all warm and fuzzy inside. Sites are plastered with quotes intended to provoke thought and inspire brotherhood of mankind. Signs that are always present but always forgotten as soon as he logs out.

Occasionally, he is allowed a glimpse of some good deed or motivating story on the news or in the papers but they don't really get the recognition they should. All the crap that happens in the world is where the news is at, that seems to be what people want to know about more. So over the years it has been determined what sells most, sex and crap.

Fluff pieces that are supposed to make Joe feel better are temporary lapses to attempt balance from all of the crap so he can get back to the crap with a fresh view. Maybe that's what keeps him sane...ish. Although, how many of those stories prompt others to do good deeds of their own? Hard to say really, not every good deed is going to be reported but Joe can bet they will fit in as many bad deed stories they can. Well, depending on their severity. A story about an extremist beheading a person will rank higher on the crappy event-o-meter than a convenient store robbery shooting. Drama wins...

Joe read somewhere the first Canadian newspaper was printed in Halifax in 1752. That's a long time to master the skill of manipulation. Maybe not that paper specifically but rather the world of journalism as a whole. Perhaps, as Joe skims over the first page from that first print, it appears the concept of the paper was to indeed, print the daily events from the time. Which were not even current, there was a story about an attack on the Pope that was 7 months old. Articles were not just local affairs, but stories from London were included as well. Apparently, just to keep people informed of the world around them. That is so weird!

It would likely take a more involved historian than Joe to attempt to conclude how the more sinister events would eventually take precedence in the entire world of journalism. Did the populous ask for them or did journalism discover they could influence perceptions and attitudes with directed media? Or, did a few dark stories and lack of interest in fluff pieces spark the interest of the populous and nurture the demand for destruction and dirty laundry? Interestingly, perhaps the hoity-toity mannerisms of the upper class harbored a secret fetish for the underworld of mischief and mayhem. Regardless of how it started, it sure evolved to a new understanding of how to direct attitudes and influence perceptions and opinions on any given topic. Perhaps the word Joe is searching for is propaganda.

He sees how easy it is today to post a billboard or a video or even just a simple picture and new thoughts on the topic are almost immediately generated. For example, if a picture is shown of a healthy person holding a banana with the words, 'bananas are healthy', you quickly believe bananas are good for you because the person in the picture looks good and the next time you go shopping for groceries the chances are better you may buy bananas. Likewise, if you were shown a picture of a banana being seductively inserted into a woman's mouth with the caption, 'bananas are proven to improve your sex drive', well, if you're a guy, chances have skyrocketed that some grocers are running out of bananas. See how easy it is to change the perception of a banana? Joe may think of that next time he watches a presidential campaign...

Mankind has always had a pecking order, a hierarchy of status where everyone tries to place themselves within the social ladder. It is evident in every stage and every walk of life. Early man adapted from the animal kingdom the 'leader of the pack' system where the strongest fight over control and the winner is supposed to see to the best interest and protection of the pack. A concept that hasn't much changed. Only now man doesn't fight, he votes and he hopes the strong winner sees to the best interest and protection of the pack. But even from those humble beginnings Joe will instinctively take on the idea that this leader is so much more important than everybody else in the pack. Leaders come and go, they get replaced by the next challenger. Think of the math, Joe. There is one leader and far more than one in the pack - who is stronger? The smart leader knows that if the pack can be kept un-unified, it is much easier to single out individual troublemakers for the smart leader also knows that a unified pack will act as a single unit that is much stronger than he is. That's not to blatantly say that there is no place for leadership - if it works. There are just so few methods that work currently because they are mostly about power and control.

But the idea of this hierarchy, where everyone wants to climb to the top because that's where the power is. Life is easier at the top. Power is exercised and control is delegated through those lower down the pole. The hierarchy involves levels and each level has its own attitude about things. If Joe wants to move up the ladder he needs to adapt his beliefs and outlook of the world to conform to the order he wishes to belong. To get to that rung, he becomes very easy to influence otherwise he won't fit in, he won't be accepted and he won't move up. Once he has moved up, then everyone on the last rung has become less than him. After accepting and living that attitude, he has successfully discarded them and changed who he is to be where he is. And Joe will change again to move further. The guy at the top, well he's all powerful, he controls everything and if Joe wants to fit in to his space, he better do everything Joe is told to do and he's allowed to do that because Joe has accepted him as the leader. Doesn't seem to matter if he's right or wrong. Joe has to accept it.

Mankind has become far too accustomed to

accepting and have only recently begun to seriously question if the whole package really fits. Mainstream media has grown so large and so obvious the veil thins to hint as to what has been going on behind the scenes. With such an ability to take pictures and video with equipment kept in pockets, journalism can report the event in the manner they see fit (or are instructed to) but the uncut story lives and breathes in all its truth and glory on social media. Joe sees firsthand that the edited version is made to look very askew to the original and the story has a completely different feel to it. Now his eyebrows squish together in that manner that shows his gears are turning.

Joe is waking up and the realization is making him grow up.

Crock Of Sh!t

NOTICE

REGISTRATION REQUIRED

Joe was a good kid. He has good parents who brought him up to be a good person. They taught him what he needed to know - finish school, get a job, get married, have kids then retire so he can enjoy his life. And that's the plan he set for himself. He finished school, got a good job at a reputable oilfield company (save for dealing with Bill) and settled into a nice house. His savings account grows a little more every month but not as much as he would like because paying the mortgage, car loan, and credit cards on top of utilities, insurance for everything and the costs of day-to-day living, money can get a little tight sometimes. Plus, the car breaks down every so often or needs new tires and he has to dip into his savings to pay for it all. Life is full of unexpected expenses and sometimes at the end of the month, he feels like he is going backwards. But he hates going to work and he hates paying all those bills. Why can't he take his hard earned money and do more things for himself? Seems like he's always giving it away to someone else and just when he thinks he's getting ahead a little bit, the taxes go up, the insurance premiums go up, the cost of living goes up.

He knows any day now he could be the next to suffer another round of cutbacks and he is unsure how he will make ends meet. He stresses about what will happen if misses his payments. His house gets taken away, his car gets repoed and he loses everything he has worked for up to this point. Taken back by the system he has spent his life supporting.

Well that's just not fair, he thinks.

Armed with an insatiable need to know, Joe sits down at his laptop, cracks himself a cold one and find this really interesting website put up by the Government of Canada called Justice Laws Website he found at *http://laws.justice.gc.ca/eng/acts*. There are all sorts of documents where he can read up on like The Universal Declaration of Human Rights, International Covenant on Social and Cultural Rights, International Covenant on Civil and Political Rights, Citizen Act, Interpretation Act, to name a few.

In particular, Joe opens up The Universal Declaration of Human Rights and learns it was adopted by the United Nations in December of 1948. For such an important document that was drafted to protect the welfare of the people, the system sure regards it as hogwash. Maybe it was scribed to appease the masses and lull them into a sense of security but doesn't really mean anything when it comes to brass taxes.

Joe cocks an eyebrow. The idea actually raises a question or two. Why was it necessary to create it in the first place? It should be understood that love, life and liberty are God-given rights blessed upon all living things. It says so in the UDoHR.

Article 1: *All human beings are born free and equal in dignity and rights. They are endowed with reason and conscience and should act towards one another in a spirit of brotherhood.*

And since this declaration was written by humans, should it not read, ***We*** *are endowed...*? Nothing has the power or authority to take anyone's dignity and God-given rights away. The declaration was accepted by the United Nations *of man*, supposedly to prevent ruling bodies and acts of terrorism to strip *man* of these rights. Therefore - what is *man* needing protection from? If a terrorist group exerts terror on another country, should it be up to the harmed country to bring these terrorists to justice or should the responsibility fall upon the shoulders of the attacking country's government if that country is part of the United Nations? That scenario makes sense to have the UDoHR. After that, the only body left with the assumed power to commit such atrocities against God is the government. Also the only assumed authority to blatantly override any such documents written by man. Never mind what may have been said in the Bible about 'all men are created equal', never mind the ten commandments - the simplest set of rules and all that is ever needed to live by, being of religious faith or not; such things seem trivial nuisances to obstruct what the power is trying to accomplish.

For the benefit of mankind...

Absolute power corrupts absolutely. Obvious details such as this and many similar have been quoted over and over for years and acknowledged, but disregarded. 'We know this is how it is but we can't change it.' So says the larger body to convince itself it isn't worth trying.

'What's the use?'

'What's the point?'

'Why bother?'

'What a crock!', Joe says and takes another

drought on his beer. Men have been corrupted because he has allowed himself to have been done so. He has allowed the system to become overbearing and too big for its britches. They have all the confidence because they have become weaponized and can only control through fear. If control has to be obtained through fear then any attempts at maintaining that control will be futile over the long term unless the fear tactics are amped up progressively to accommodate the people's complacency to them.

But this is taught from early on. Mankind's humble beginnings were started with fear based tactics. The leader of the pack dominated through fear. Aggression seized the position, aggression keeps it and if anyone objected they got killed, severely beaten and banished from the pack - or they fight for authority to get their voice heard. Time passes and the authority becomes a king and queen and a following of lesser beings called dukes and earls and whatnot, such people are the assumed voice of the people to aid the decisions of the king and queen who have lost touch with reality and the ways of 'commoners'. They live in castles and everything from bathing, eating, dressing to removing bed pans were tasks done by someone else. The posh lifestyle divided them from understanding what living was all about and they were given that power, mankind let them believe they were more important because of their position, mankind let that power corrupt. Who then would make the better leader, he who has no concept of struggling to survive or he who has struggled and understands why there should not be need for struggle?

Fast forward again to man's present hierarchy. Here, there have been created titles called president, prime minister, premier, governor, joint chiefs of staff, mayor, council(person)... the branches seem endless. Everybody has to have a title to give them meaning to their existence and with that title comes entitlements, like tax breaks. Joe wonders how important that must make them feel. They should feel more responsible to make sure the rest of us are doing okay with our lives. After all, these folks are voted in, if they don't do their jobs properly they don't get to keep their jobs on the next vote. Right? That's how it is supposed to work?

Prime Minister: *the head of an elected government; the principal minister of a sovereign or state.*

Sovereign: *possessing supreme or ultimate power.*

UDoHR, Article 2: *Everyone is entitled to all the rights and freedoms set forth in this Declaration, without* *distinction of any kind, such as race, colour, sex, language, religion, political or other opinion, national or social origin, property, birth or other status. Furthermore, no distinction shall be made on the basis of the political, jurisdictional or international status of the country or territory to which a person belongs, whether it be independent, trust, non-self-governing or under any other limitation of sovereignty.*

This looks contradicting, thinks Joe. If everyone is entitled to all the rights and freedoms set forth, why are those fancy titled people getting so much more than the common people? And how can sovereignty possess supreme or ultimate power but be labelled as having limitations? If sovereignty truly has no limitations in its ultimate power, then there is nothing, absolutely nothing, to prohibit the entitlement to all the rights and freedoms set forth. Yet the 'sovereign', at the time of this writing, has been stripping away rights and freedoms by destroying jobs and securities. Less money coming back to the homes and families, more money going out to the system. This is looking out for the best interests of the people? This is entitling the people to anything promised in the UDoHR? After a hardworking citizen has lost their job due to work shortage, run out of their employment insurance benefits, would it be possible to square off with the 'sovereign' and cite:

Article 25, section 1: *Everyone has the right to a standard of living adequate for the health and well-being of himself and of his family, including food, clothing, housing and medical care and necessary social services, and the right to security in the event of unemployment, sickness, disability, widowhood, old age or other lack of livelihood in circumstances beyond his control.*

Joe should have nothing to worry about. If he loses his job - because of decisions made by his elected officials - he should be entitled to the security of his basic needs of life, right? He has the right to security and it should not be for a set amount of (short) time based on what he has had to pay into it in the first place. He should be entitled to those securities until he can support himself again. But instead, there are packages and plans available for income support - if you are eligible to qualify - and very confusing to find and read through and on a limited time offer. It all appears to be substandard in return for the amount Joe pays into it and it screams 'try to fix your situation yourself as best you can, we're mostly here to collect'. Keeping Joe reliant on the system keeps the system in power.

Wait Joe, maybe this is being interpreted wrong. Who provides the security? That is not clearly defined. Surely it must be the 'sovereign' as circumstances beyond the workers control caused the unemployment. However, he knows most will argue that is the people's taxes and regular deductions from his paychecks that provide the funds for his securities. Perhaps if the government didn't have to put so much money into military development or politician's salaries... But, with all means of income cut off, there is no other option but to go to those who are elected and sworn in to see that the benefits and the needs of the people are met.

Or... new communities are sprouted with a vision to shed the reliance on a system that has failed them and become self-sufficient. It's already happening.

The fundamental rights of the free human being are not exercised, they are being ignored. The next generation suffers more as this hierarchy is indoctrinated into our children when they go to school. They are taught adults have power over them as guardians, teachers, instructors, principals, councilors; each must be listened to and obeyed. After all, their safety is at stake, they are incapable of making rational decisions on their own so a controlling body must be established to do it for them. Sound familiar? Look at the changes in the course curriculum. It's not about getting the right answer anymore, it's about getting the answer as instructed.

What happens then if the much larger group, 'the people', ask the 'sovereign' why they are the very same who counteract article 30?

Nothing in this Declaration may be interpreted as implying for any State, group or person any right to engage in any activity or to perform any act aimed at the destruction of any of the rights and freedoms set forth herein.

The 'sovereign' are people too, a State or group of them, but human beings nonetheless who are awarding themselves additional freedoms and securities at the cost of 'the people', nay, while 'the people' suffer unnecessary hardship.

Joe wants to know who governs the governors? Who steps up and says, 'Hey, something isn't right here!' Well nobody, we aren't allowed to do that, never mind that **Article 19** states:

Everyone has the right to freedom and expression; this right includes freedom to hold opinions without interference and to seek, receive and impart information and ideas through any media and regardless of frontiers.

Or **Article 29, section 2:** *In the exercise of his rights and freedoms, everyone shall be subject only to such limitations as are determined by law solely for the purpose of securing due recognition and respect for the rights and* *freedoms of others and of meeting the just requirements of morality, public order and the general welfare in a democratic society.*

That article should mean if someone chooses to uphold the rights and freedoms of others, meeting the just requirements, the 'sovereign' should not be allowed to shut said someone up and:

Article 9: *No one shall be subjected to arbitrary arrest, detention or exile.*

...in a democratic system. But Joe begins to wonder if that is what is maintained today?

Democracy, Merriam-Webster: 1. *a: government by the people; especially: rule of the majority. b: a government in which the supreme power is vested in the people and exercised by them directly or indirectly through a system of representation usually involving periodically held free elections. 2. a political unit that has a democratic government.*

So we get to vote our leaders in as our representatives and they should govern according to our best interests, with our voice being taken into strong consideration. They are our voice in parliament, but it remains to be seen that there is anything being accomplished 'by the people'. Joe leans back in his chair for a moment. Is that it? Is that how it's supposed to be? Lately, they decided all on their own to shut down the oil and gas industry in western Canada and Joe is about to lose his job, they decided to change the education system, they decided to force carbon tax, they decided to bring in thousands of immigrants and change the laws and culture to suit them, they decided to send millions of dollars to other countries to support their economies, they decided to regulate where certain items can be purchased from (gypsum, for example). The distinctive Canadian uniforms have been changed, the national anthem, Merry Christmas, the Lord's Prayer... what Joe sees is a collapse of culture and economy and Joe's opinion seems not to be a contributing factor. There is something more familiar in this style of governing and Joe scrambles to look it up:

Communism, The Free Dictionary: *A system of government in which the state plans and controls the economy and a single, often authoritarian party holds power, claiming to make progress toward a higher social order in which all goods are equally shared by the people.*

Joe notices the word, 'claiming'. Progress is

indisputably being made in this age, it is just unclear that the underlying goal and outcome is equally shared. This is where the 'sovereign' wants us to be...?

Yet the system can't be held entirely responsible for the current state of things. Everybody let it happen. Everybody allowed it. As carefully planned and orchestrated as it may have been over the years, everybody is responsible for letting things get to this point. Naturally, when those in power get what they want, they push harder and for more. When they get that, the cycle continues and never really stops until it is stopped. How does such a beast get stopped? They can threaten with guns and retribution, penalties and incarceration - but that's oppression is it not? That's willfully ignoring Article 9 because the people chose to act on Article 19. Even the gunner with his hand on the trigger must come to reason when the order from his superiors is beyond the comprehension of sensibility.

That bears repeating - **Even the gunner with his hand on the trigger must come to reason when the order from his superiors is beyond the comprehension of sensibility.**

Somewhere, somehow, someone has to change their mind. The 'sovereign' do not squeeze triggers, they order someone else to do it. For them, faceless victims make it easier to sleep at night and that is the value everybody has been whittled down to, faceless victims, numbers on an electronic document - a source of income. Expendable assets if you will. A few generations of such behaviour and the people have become submissive. The 'sovereign' cannot be questioned because their retribution will be swift and those questioning will be made examples of for future people with thoughts of questioning. Well that's not very democratic, Joe. Lately, there have been those questioning, those realizing 'the world doesn't make sense' and those voices must have spread for there have been changes in the system. An economy suffers and people have less, an education system is re-evaluated and changed with new ways to do things, unreasonable methods to solve equations and answers are accepted because they were completed following specific steps, not that they were done and correct. Methodology overshadows creativity with an underlying motive to turn children into conforming citizens and ensure they do not grow to be intelligent, free-thinkers who may one day question the 'sovereign'. Teach them to do as instructed, to obey.

And upon successfully completing that system, people like Joe are obliged to enter another - the work force. By doing so, his time is traded for money and doing as instructed is continued for the benefit of the employer while Joe maintains a **J**ust **O**ver **B**roke status in most cases. Joe has a good income but mandatory systems are in place to strip him of much of that income - insurance, driver's license fees, taxes, registration, interest, more taxes...

Did you know - **Article 13, section 1:** *Everyone has the right to freedom of movement and residence within the borders of each State.*

That seems to make driver's licenses obsolete does it not? Joe may review section 1 and think that it says 'freedom of movement', meaning, 'to move freely' which would justify the legality of regular payments for a driver's license but if Joe does not have said permission slip, he has to find another means of movement, which makes his ability to move restricted. Coupled with mandatory vehicle registration and insurance (yes, insurance is good to have to cover accident costs, Joe does not dispute that), his movement is restricted more so taking away his *freedom of movement.*

Some do find wealth and a measure of fulfillment and that's a promising thing. But for Joe, he has to justify his existence by get up, go to work, go home, eat-sleep-repeat. A few weeks per year for a holiday and hopefully on weekends and stat holidays those pet projects he has like fix up the classic car stuck in the garage may take another step toward completion. This may not be the way of life intended for him by any religion, it is what was built and it is corrupt and only teaches corruptive behaviour. Joe has been taught to lie, cheat and steal in pursuit of more - more wealth, more power, more stuff. Such things entertain an unsatisfied ego, not a hungry soul looking to be nurtured.

This is the system that was created. It was bred through the lust for power and control and the question remains if there is not a better way. Mankind is not advancing as a human race, not mentally, not spiritually, not even intelligently.

Scared As Sh!t

NOTICE

MUST BE ACCOMPANIED BY AN ADULT

One day, Joe goes to work feeling more nervous than usual. He was called to his company's Human Resources office instead of the meeting shack on site. The news was given, he is laid off. He has severance pay to carry him over a couple of weeks but he is going have to find something else soon. After packing up what belongings he had, Joe drives himself home in a delirium of shock. What now?

His skill set revolved around oilfield and there either aren't too many of those jobs to go to or there are too many other qualified people applying. The outlook is grim. He starts the process of employment insurance, at least he would have almost a year of lower income to manage things with. Sitting at home on his laptop filling out the forms for his benefits, Joe is flooded with the anger of the unfairness of it all. The only reason he was suddenly out of work was because the oil and gas industry was forced to collapse. The only reason he couldn't save up enough of a nest egg to carry him through tough times was all of life's expenses to take care of on a limited income. Everything he put into the system and he is to only get a fraction of what he needs back, for a limited time.

He wants to scream at his 'representative' for equal benefits in times of hardship. He wants to tell him the system isn't fair and he wants everybody to hear it. But, like reporting Bill to management, retribution might be swift and harsh. He's seen stories about what happens to conspiracy theorists and nay-sayers of the system. They disappear. So Joe does the next logical step, he begins to research what the system is made of and how he can turn it to his advantage. To take back some of what was his to start with.

Every aspect of his life has him scared to move or say anything out of place. Fear kept Joe from speaking against Bill's behaviour for his job may have been terminated as a result. Fear keeps Joe from sharing certain opinions amongst society or his peers for his character may be shunned as outcast. And, fear keeps Joe from questioning the 'sovereign' for his life may be incarcerated or terminated if he learns too much and speaks too loudly.

'Not possible', some would protest. History, however, is littered with notable and influential people who have died 'under mysterious circumstance' which rules possibility as a moot point until proven otherwise. Stories and theories continue to surface and they always will as long as someone finds a reason to discredit or quiet someone else who is opposing a belief or goal.

Fear controls. Fear makes folk submissive. Even on the school playground this theory is tested regularly when the bully uses fear to overpower the smaller and weaker. The system knows this all too well. Fear is best backed by the right tools and Joe has learned, he who holds the bigger gun, strikes the most fear. But if the military builds a bigger gun as a deterrent against threat from another country it just incites a pissing contest. It returns man to the school ground, 'mine's bigger than yours' contest. Maybe the world's armouries are developed less for outside attack and more for inside uprising. Control can only be managed for so long. Eventually the chain gets too short and the dog goes wild.

Every ancient society ever having power did so based on fear tactics. Rule and power expanded through warfare and conquest of other cultures and societies and those beaten were inducted into the winner's belief system. Those who did not assimilate were killed. Such a means worked for conquering new peoples and building an empire but what means were used to maintain control? Constant warmongering worked for a while. People feared war and being forcibly removed from their wealth, home and lifestyle or being killed in battle. But talking about the possibility of impending war loses its luster after a time. People come to believe that it won't happen so an actual war is created to put that fear back into them.

Over time, many cultures learned to use religion to 'put the fear of God' in their subjects. What greater sense of fear can be had than the wrath of a deity who could smite thee in the blink of an eye, or unleash plagues upon the land? And even in the afterlife, should a subject not please his ruler his eternal soul would suffer damnation. The Egyptian rulers did it by proclaiming themselves gods for centuries. Indeed very powerful motives to enforce submission.

With the eventual need of new ideas to maintain control in changing times came a sneaky and very dark structure. The government preyed on the vulnerabilities of Joe by informing him of various threats against his way of life. Threats, both external and internal and ever present, then they would swoop in to save the day as the great protectors. There would always be another sinister threat lurking in the shadows waiting to strike and there would always be another press conference where an elected official would stand up before Joe to declare that such actions would not be tolerated on Joe's soil! And the worst, if any such attacks were actually proven to be orchestrated, Joe would face the cold reality that his government openly murders its own for the sake of perpetuating the fear control system. Uh oh, that makes Joe's government the real terrorists... They keep the fear in the people and profit from arms deals in the process.

But the officials would not save Joe against real or imagined doom for his safety, they would do so to fan the flames of their designs for control. To this day does Joe not see an onslaught of stories warning him of all sorts of disasters? All at once he faces global destruction through obesity, another drug that is killing teenagers, another bug or infected animal, a new disease or disorder that has to be treated but not until a few to several people have died from it, another terrorist group threatening his life and attacking his city followed by several stories of how the attack was orchestrated, even the moon landing was claimed to be falsified. Honey bees are dropping dead, the very climate is turning against him, killer clowns are wandering his streets and people actually believe a zombie apocalypse is a real threat! Clowns and zombies... imagine!

How afraid of terrorist attacks was the population prior to 9/11? How many threats have been publicized since? How afraid were farmers of mad cow disease and how many new outbreaks of various strains have popped up since? Why is mankind suffering from stronger flu viruses only over the last 10 years or so? How long has flesh eating disease (or Necrotizing Fasciitis) been around? It only seems to attack folks with weaker immune systems and such people are more common because more pills are prescribed to combat anything. Chemically produced medicines are known to weaken the immune system because they do not force the body to fend for itself. And doctors are paid commission to push more drugs... Fear of the next virus that will kill Joe ensues so he must immunize and take those prescribed meds as directed so he will become more susceptible to the viruses.

Case in point: a healthy person and a dead person do not make the system more money.

When the next hint of threats arise, Joe will look to his fearless leaders for protection with all the vigour of an automated response. The Wizard of Oz was the best example of this idea - Joe believes there is an all-powerful wizard looking over him but it's just a simple, although very creative, man behind a curtain. Joe is so easily convinced of anything. The right commercial in the right place, a believable storyline in a movie, consistent articles or commentary in the news, directed sleight of hand and misdirection in advertising, not to mention - if a celebrity believes it, it must be real. Alone, Joe might be able to figure things out logically. Place him in a group, and that group is dumb as sh!t.

Why wouldn't the mass media moguls and curators have all good reason to report what the government tells them to report? Would they not twice benefit from the agreement? Once to gain Joe as an active audience who pays the bills and second to remain safe from any such government retribution and continue to operate in a profitable manner. Another opportunity for the officials to exercise control with a 'play along or else' speech.

In due course, the supreme rulers devised a method to 'give power to the people', a shameless scam they labelled democracy. And Joe bought it. Joe believes that just because he votes in his elected officials, he has the power to control the way those officials act in parliament. Does he? Has anybody stood up and asked for the astronomical job loss in western Canada? Or voted in favour of changing dress codes, the national anthem, or the Lord's Prayer? Did anybody put a stop to millions of support money going to other countries to support their economy while his continues to suffer? That still looks like the officials do whatever they want after they get in. Proof that candidates make many promises to get elected but are thick with excuses why those promises can't be upheld. Most of them anyway, there are a few who try harder.

Eventually, new branches of government began to spring up to combat internal threats in the name of social securities. Certain benefits and insurances were put into place to protect Joe from the likes of illness, job loss, disability, disaster, old age, etc... Such services they were so thoughtful to set for our benefit, but make Joe pay for. Joe won't get employment insurance without having paid into it first. And he better get laid off, not fired or quit for then it's his fault he is unemployed and not entitled. It reads like an insurance company finding tiny details and excuses to not pay out. Joe could have worked twenty years with regular deposits into the system but he will only get a percent of it back spread out in equal payments over the course of less than one year. He will work his entire life in hopes that a pittance of a pension will still be there when he retires. But Joe's elected official, well he gets tax breaks, free housing, servants, free services, an exorbitant income and a more than healthy pension after just four years. Get voted in early, retire early and he never has to work again. All for not doing what Joe asked him to do in the first place. Such things would fuel Joe's dislike for the system.

And why not? He now lives in a welfare state. convinced that the government is protecting him from every imaginable fear they can create. They take every measure imaginable to justify their excuses to invade Joe's privacy and strip him of his rights and freedoms. They can spend money on warfare to counter the proposed threat of military invasion. They can spend money on heightened security systems to counter the proposed threat of terrorist attack. They can spend money on surveys and studies to tell Joe the planet is not collapsing, it's just a shift in weather patterns. They can also spend money on media coverage to draw Joe's focus to whatever fear tactic they need him to pay attention to in efforts to draw him away from something they are trying to cover up. All of which justifies demanding Joe's tax dollars.

Joe begins to understand the more the government tightens its grip on public and private services, the more control they are amassing over his entire life. Through that control they can turn everything on the planet to their advantage. They can take what they want, do what they want with complete disregard for the quality of Joe's life. They tell him to be loyal and patriotic while they systematically dismember every ounce of freedom he has left until he no longer feels human, he is cattle, corralled into an existence of slavery to a greater power.

UDoHR, Article 4: *No one shall be held in slavery or servitude; slavery and the slave trade shall be prohibited in all their forms.*

Take A Sh!t

Joe might be feeling close to hitting the bottom. He doesn't have much for savings but what he has should get him through for a month which is how long employment insurance will take to start paying. What does he do after that? If he can't get back to work how is he supposed to provide himself with his basic necessities? EI pays enough to cover some expenses but he will eventually have to figure out where to cancel some monthly utilities he can do without. Now he is no longer able to live within the standard and quality of life he built for himself. If Joe's downward cycle continues he will manifest psychological issues that his survival mode will learn to cope with by taking what he needs to maintain himself.

Initiate social disorder.

Joe's need to survive, or fight-or-flight mode, will change his views on consequence and social behaviours. He may not think twice about taking something from someone else in the name of self-preservation. With many people in Joe's situation taking the same outlook on life, the consequence leads to social degradation and eventual economic collapse. Economically, every time someone steals property from a business or private owner, something has to offset that loss. Prices increase not only to attempt to recoup but now security measures have to be increased. The installation of cameras or a beefier security system, staff, monthly expenses, insurance premiums for making the claim; all factors added in so next time, either the crime is prevented before it happens or the merchandize is recovered afterward.

Returning the owners property is always a gratifying feeling. The owners is relieved their stuff is back safe and sound and the police are satisfied they have another criminal off the streets. But that means that criminal has to be prosecuted and sent through the court system and possibly incarcerated on taxpayers' money. With an overwhelming amount of criminals being processed, there will be a greater demand for money to process them. Higher consumer prices, higher taxes for everybody, there is no win-win under such conditions.

The social impact can be even more devastating. Dog-eat-dog becomes a defined expression as personal items become more valued and hoarded. They are hard earned and not easily shared for fear of them not being returned. That leads to trust issues amongst friends, neighbours and workmates, paranoia and constant suspicion which amplifies distrust. Joe's motives to protect his property now justifies his ownership of a gun. Ownership of a gun now gives Joe the power to go take something if his survival mode demands it.

Taking things is a primal notion. It usually requires power and control to do it effectively. For Joe to just take something he would have to have control over himself to ignore the consequences of his actions, or he would need power over others to take it without consequence. A gun seems to make Joe's attitude toward the matter easier to deal with. Either way, taking anything from anybody has negative connotations behind it. Taking things is a selfish pursuit to please the id part of egotism and reflects an unchecked intellect feeding primal instincts. Joe has other research on that...

Over the long term, communities become separated and families become isolated. Joe will not make an effort to socialize with people he does not trust for that may lead to an opportunity to be stolen from. Joe's suspicions cause him to behave in manners not conforming to regular social etiquettes which causes his neighbours to become suspicious of him. Round and round the world turns, always feeding on the blights of decent society. One person steals from another depleting them of their 'stock', that person in turn may have to steal from another to replenish that stock and so on...

Hate is fed in this manner. Social biases against race, age and appearance are assumed and acted upon. Wrongfully accused, a person will harbour ill intent on his accusers and he may choose to act out against those people, further justifying the accuser's claims and not helping the person who was unfairly accused in the first place. A vicious cycle of torment and negative feedback.

What of the corporate moguls who become richer on profits derived from carefully assembled ad campaigns that convince Joe to buy stuff he doesn't need? They convince Joe he needs it and by doing so the corporations can drive the need for any market or any product. They feed on Joe's gullibility. In return they provide shoddy products backed by limited service, sell it off as a good deal then take Joe's money. Products get made cheaper, they are designed to break down yet the costs keep going up perpetually feeding Joe's need to steal the product when he can't afford to buy it. The rich keep getting richer... Gone are the days when quality counted for something, it's not something that is very often even guaranteed anymore. They can't guarantee the product, they know it's sh!t, they aren't concerned about the quality of said product, they are only concerned with getting the money for said product. That's taking something else from Joe, they are taking him for granted.

But money and personal belongings aren't all that is taken from Joe. People have figured out how to take his lifestyle, his dignity and even his identity. Without a job and a means to support himself, Joe's purpose and self-worth withers away leaving a husk of a human being begging for handouts from the system that was supposed to be developed to make sure he had everything he needed in the first place. Is there a greater loss of dignity than having to beg for scraps because Joe is not able to provide for himself?

He can flip through his wallet and things suddenly become clearer to him. His entire life has been digitized and imprinted onto tiny plastic cards. The sum of his existence staring back at him from capital letters to identify him, categorize him, give him permission to do things and give him access to his own money. Inside this hand-sized leather pouch is the ability to steal who Joe is. In the hands of the wrong people, Joe would cease to exist and yet be born in another form with another face at the same time. Imagine what Joe would have to go through, the process and explanation of trying to prove to the system he really is Joe. The system that created him in the first place and digitized him into plastic and numbers that would not comprehend Joe's face, mind, body and soul belong to him and no one else. How many people would he have to bring before the system would accept his word?

Strange, he thinks to himself, how easy it has become to devalue a human being when he is downsized from flesh and blood into a two inch by three inch polymer compound. Joe wonders if the name on the cards, the all capital letter name is really him after all. The name does not match his signature with only the first letters in upper case. Joe remembers something from his high school social class about political sciences, an interesting conversation his teacher had brought up and he began to research.

Diving into corporate law, Joe discovers that a human being, consisting of mind, body and soul was created by God and given free-will by Him and thus cannot be controlled by another human being, group, corporation, governing body or ruler. Well that throws a wrench into the machinations of political power, thinks Joe. How does the system have such control over him then?

Barron's Canadian Law Dictionary, fourth edition (ISBN 0-7641-0616-3):
•***natural person.*** *A natural person is a human being that has the capacity for rights and duties.*
•***artificial person.*** *A legal entity, not a human being, recognized as a person in law to whom certain legal rights and duties may attached - e.g. a body corporate.*

In order for the system to clean things up and make things run smoothly, the definitions for corporation, person, natural person, artificial person, individual, and so forth are re-defined to suit the particular covenant, act or declaration for the benefit of the system's purpose. Joe thinks that is very odd, how can a word or phrase mean one thing in one document then mean the complete opposite in another document? One word - convenience.

Diving in further, Joe realizes in order for the system to 'own' something, it plays God and creates it. The system knows the creator owns the property it has created so it devised a method to exact the same power: corporations, and thus was born the artificial person in all capital letters. This is Joe's digital copy, the corporate entity the system owns and has control over. The system can demand anything it wants from this 'person' because the system created it. Now Joe realizes why the capital letter person is on every government issued form of identification. In order for them to hold Joe the human being accountable for the actions of JOE the legal entity, they tricked him into believing they are one in the same person and make it law with his signature on every document. It's not difficult for him to piece together which document that legally declared him as a corporation into the system - his birth certificate. The system declares no one is of sound mind to enter into any contract until the age of eighteen, until then, the signing of such documents need to be signed by a guardian. Since Joe's parents had no idea what they were actually signing and being informed that they legally have to register Joe into existence, of course they signed the birth certificate legally declaring Joe as an asset and controllable entity to the system.

Every corporation has to be assigned a business number in order to conduct business so Joe's parents happily and unknowingly obliged to the system's demand of getting him a social insurance number. Now the system can monitor every move Joe makes because he needs his SIN to get a driver's license, bank account, passport, credit card, mortgage, and the system can step in and claim ownership over any property Joe accumulates because Joe doesn't actually own anything, JOE does and the system owns JOE. Convenient - golly, there's that word again.

There are the three parts that make Joe a functioning corporation the system uses to do business with in the corporate world: a **CORPORATE NAME**, a business number and an officer acting on behalf of the JOE corporation. This is entity, the faceless being, that holds more value and worth then Joe the human being and why anyone would want to take his identity in the first place. That's exactly what the system did. They took Joe's identity, his natural person to create an artificial person they can control.

The fact that Joe was unknowingly entered into such a contract, without his, or his guardians' awareness and understanding of the terms and conditions of the contract, makes it null and void. Well now Joe just wants to throw his hands up in the air and scream, "Screw you system, I'm out!".

BUT.

The system is smarter than that. It has had a long time to fill in the gaps and refine their process. Joe has to be reliant on the system. To facilitate his basic needs he must have shelter, warmth, food and water - and a means to pay for it all. A house is very expensive and he must enter into a contract with lending outfit to get the funds to pay for it. To heat and power his house he must enter into a contract with service providers and to eat and drink he must pay for groceries and store them so they don't rot before he can consume them. To pay for all of these necessities, Joe must have a job, which he provides his SIN so his income can be tracked and taken if needed (garnisheed) and in order to get to work he needs a vehicle. He may need a loan to pay for the car, the system demands he register and insure it and to top it off, he needs his permission slip (driver's permit) to go anywhere. How does Joe fulfill his *right to a standard of living adequate for the health and well-being of himself and of his family, including food, clothing, housing and medical care and necessary social services, and the right to security in the event of unemployment, sickness, disability, widowhood, old age or other lack of livelihood in circumstances beyond his control* without the permission of the system? The system took that too.

Convenient...

All of this leads Joe to one more thought, how did the system take control of money? He does some more research about the value of money and learns that our fiat monetary system is not based on the fact that money has no value at all. It hasn't since 1933 when at the time of the Great Depression the US and Canada (and eventually everyone else) declared bankruptcy. It was declared then that money was no longer to be backed by gold or silver. Since the founding fathers declared only gold and silver can be money but that can be a burden to carry large sums of coins around, the coupon was developed to make it easier. These were traded as promissory notes where the person who received one in exchange for goods or services would take it to the bank and the bank would give back the amount on the note in gold or silver. Effective and a win/win for everybody.

FDR's Executive Order 6102, signed on April 5, 1933, forbade anyone to hoard gold coin, bullion and certificates but he modified that act in March with Presidential Proclamation 2039 to forbid 'gold or silver coin or bullion or currency'. It was all wrapped up with a hefty penalty of $10 000 and/or up to five to ten years incarceration. Wait a minute, Joe thinks out loud. The government is claiming no individual, partnership, association or corporation can hoard money yet the government is counted as a corporation. Joe does not live in the country of Canada or the United States of America, he lives within the boundaries of the corporate entity of Canada or the United States of America. That corporation took back all but a small amount of the people's money and kept it someplace safe, thereby hoarding it themselves but of course, no one questions because they make the rules and that money has to go somewhere, right?

So Joe investigates further. Before the depression while gold and silver did back the coupons, the Federal Reserve notes had to have 40% of gold backing and by the late 20's, the credit limit on the notes had pretty much ran out. Executive Order 6102 prevented the Federal reserve from increasing the money supply which actually worsened the depression. Makes sense, no one can own gold so notes could not be redeemed and no more notes could be made, basic supply and demand.

The Great Depression lasted ten years (1929-1939), still effecting countries until the beginning of WWII. There is a pause in Joe's research as he postulates a theory. He reaches for a pen and paper and jots down a series of events.

> Reserve notes lost backing by the late 20's
> A recession began, confidence in investments dropped
> Recession turned into depression
> Possession of gold and silver declared illegal
> Depression got worse
> World War II started
> Economy boosted

Joe studies his list. He is hard pressed not to wonder if the events were not instigated and initiated for a greater purpose. It seems to have worked out for the benefit of the system. Today, Joe knows his money is not backed by anything of value at all. He finds a definition of fiat money:

- Any money declared by a government to be legal tender
- State-issued money which is neither convertible by law to any other thing, nor fixed in value in terms of any objective standard
- Intrinsically valueless money used as money because of government decree

Joe's 'legal tender' is nothing more than printed paper with a face value that is repeatedly traded and traded again for goods and services without anything of value being exchanged. Should the government refuse or can't guarantee the value of its legal tender then there is no value in it at all anymore. The government then has successfully taken money away from Joe and maintained the control of the flow of any currency under their power. All they have to do is threaten to do so and they create another fear within the society. Fear controls as Joe remembers.

Anybody can go dig up gold and trade that in for money but if everyone did that then there would be too much gold and the value would be decreased. Besides, it's not that easy. Searching for gold has been going on for centuries so it is unlikely anyone today would find a deposit large enough to constitute an early retirement. The government also enforces licenses for anything more than gold panning because the system knows no one will find enough dust to make a difference. Licenses required paperwork, government paperwork takes time and once permitted, if Joe was to find something of significance, they would know about it because he is registered. Wait for it...

Convenient.

Although, digging a little deeper, Joe may see gold as money because it was once used to back the value of money but gold is not money itself, as realized by an Italian Professor of Economics, Augusto Graziani. Gold, though a valuable mineral, is a resource anyone can produce for themselves. Therefore, it was only ever used as means of trading for goods placing it into a barter system, not a monetary one.

Upon recollecting what he keeps in his wallet, he notices there is far more plastic than paper. His 'money' isn't even in paper form anymore, it's digital. What is keeping digital money from being created in an infinite supply? There isn't anything of value backing it anyway so why not make enough to say, end world hunger? More research for Joe.

Ultimately, there is something of value backing money. Conventionally, Joe believes any transaction is being completed between two people, a buyer and a seller. But there actually three as Graziani pointed out; a buyer, a seller and a promiser to pay. If Joe wants to buy a new watch and pays with his debit card, the funds are withdrawn from his account, credited to the account of the watch seller and facilitated by the bank who has to promise to pay the seller by completing the transaction. It still applies when using paper legal tender because the note has to have been created and backed by the government's promise to pay, or guarantee the notes value.

Then what process actually creates money? Any money is created when the bank extends a loan. The money is not already there as a profit in the bank's records thusly having the money to fulfill the loan amount, it is created at the time the contract is signed. Joe wants a loan for $5000 to buy a new car, as soon as he adds his signature to the contract, the bank can now create the money out of thin air and add that amount to his account. This shows as an asset to the bank and a liability to

Joe. As Joe pays back the loan, with interest, the bank records each payment as another asset and the money created disappears, one payment at a time.

Ergo, since Joe has to have an income to pay back the loan, the thing of value backing the money that was created, is his labour. As long as Joe stays working and borrowing money and as long as there is enough strain on the economy so Joe is never self-reliant, the system goes round and round.

Deep Sh!t

NOTICE

AUTHORIZED PERSONNEL ONLY

When Joe wakes up the next morning he feels very much different. Not entirely because of the amount of beer he consumed being frustrated at learning how things work either. A cycle has been broken. Gone is the familiar routine of breakfast, Facebook, go to work. He skips breakfast and settles for just coffee, taking it to his chair with his phone in hand. He opens the app and browses the different posts but with a different perception than before. He can feel it but can't relate it to anything. He sees posts of people complaining about how others don't stay connected, a news video about another missing person, another video about cats and a few pictures of inspiration with a touch-your-heart phrase. Then he sees the all too familiar posts of varying media about the different opinions of the nation's leaders.

He scrolls through the posts, one after the other, sometimes watching a video if it relates to his current mood. He's at a loss now, feeling like things should be more simple when things go bad, like someone should be there to make sure he doesn't lose everything he has worked for. What does he sacrifice to make sure something else gets paid? If he shuts off the tv, how does he keep up with current events? If his power or heat is shut off... well that's just wrong, that means the system doesn't care at all if he lives or dies as long as he figures out a way to pay the bills.

There is depression, loss, hopelessness. Joe feels helpless because his standard of living is changing and there should be something he can do about it. But with the country on the threat of recession and more people losing their jobs, Joe needs to address his mental health. Being out of work can have serious negative effects on him. He's not leaving the house every day and socializing with co-workers. the loss of a job could have him feeling less of a person, striking at his very identity if he cannot support himself and has to ask for help. That sort of depression could lead to anxiety, sleeping disorders and eventually substance abuse to try to cope leading to a change in his entire personality and who he is. Joe is a fairly outgoing guy, he likes meeting new people, he's kind and polite. Prolonged unemployment and the inability to sustain himself could make him a desperate individual willing to beg and steal to survive. In turn, that would lead to paranoia of getting caught and turn Joe into an introvert, unwilling to talk to people at all because of extreme guilt and hate for what the world has done to him. He won't be the only one who suffers either, he will be easily angered and take out his stresses on family members and friends should he see them.

Fortunately, he isn't going there but imagine this effect on a larger scale, say, most of Joe's city, or province, or country. That many people out of work and struggling to survive. How many outcomes become evident at that scale? Anarchy? Complete disintegration of economic structure? The end of life as we know it? Armageddon? Would the government actually have some sort of diabolical Noah's Ark type plan to cleanse the world and remake it where they hold supreme power?

The problem Joe might postulate is in man's evolution. Meaning there hasn't been an evolutionary leap since... maybe since we learned to develop the spoken language. Modern society still performs under the same motives as the dark ages. There are rulers who seek all power and control over their subjects and will exercise any means necessary to achieve and maintain that control - fear and oppression. Evolution has been stagnant for millennia. Maybe that is not entirely true, evolution means change, doesn't matter if it's forward or backward.

For evolution for work, there needs to be an external influence in an environment to promote an internal change or mutation within an organism. Once that happens, natural selection takes over to decide which mutation takes hold and the organism adapts. Mankind has had no such external influences to force any mutations. The world has not changed. The technology has changed which has removed man from the natural world and made his environment artificial. There is an improved knowledge and ability to manipulate the physical world but the knowledge has only weakened the species. Living easier came at a price.

Physically, Joe is a weaker man with modern medicine forcing new chemical quick fixes into him so Pharma can make more money. Generations of use make for a weaker immune system and a degradation of forward evolutionary steps. Every year there seems to be another new disease or strange strand of an old one and the government is always there with promise that a cure will be discovered. More tax money is poured into research and studies to combat another fear he has to contend with. They have spewed out the same promises about cancer and muscular dystrophy. Look at the efforts of the great Jerry Lewis who, over nearly fifty years, raised 2.6 billion dollars to find a cure. What should that tell Joe? Perhaps there's more profit in searching for a cure than finding one.

Mentally, Joe is not as competent for technology is designed to do the work for him. Computations, design, labour, entertainment, even driving; nearly every responsibility of life taken over by a computer or machine. So much time on the planet to learn and discover and Joe is still only capable of accessing only ten percent of his brain function.

Spiritually, Joe has no need for the connection because the government provides all that is necessary. To reconnect with the spiritual, Joe may discover the reliance on government is not necessary for a happy existence. Spiritual growth has been overshadowed by religion and nearly abandoned in man's early development but it has resurfaced and is making a slow comeback. It's awakening in Joe because he longs to be around trees and grass. He finds himself staring at birds as they fly overhead, he is creating a new belief system for himself and he is beginning to understand the need for more freedom and less stuff.

With all this information at hand, with understanding that evolution requires a variation in species, as in humans: hereditability - the traits of change that are to be passed on, and the struggle for existence - those best suited for their environment will reproduce; Joe can figure out that man has been the conjuror of his own demise. Joe's body has been inherently designed to fail through evolution. The constant introduction of drugs, bad air and foods that are processed and genetically modified will lead to a new generation of slightly weaker human beings.

There are posts with phrases similar to, 'the quality of your thoughts reflects the quality of your life'. This has a surprising measure of truth. If Joe was to notice that when he is in a good mood for an extended period of time, things just seem to go his way. Like the universe lines everything up for his benefit. He finds a twenty in a jacket pocket he hasn't worn in a while, he hits every green light on the way to work, somebody brought extra pizza to work and shared with him. Likewise, if he is in a foul mood, everything that can go wrong, will. One day his alarm doesn't go off because of a power failure during the night. In his rush to get ready for work, he spills his coffee and needs to change his pants, then he may walk out the door and forget his car keys and he has to go back in to get them. On his way to work, yep, traffic jam. This is not an unfamiliar episode for many. Each little event compounds frustration and anger onto the next event until Joe is having a really bad day.

Joe will remember every detail about that bad day as he tells his friends about just how bad it was because that feeds into the doom and gloom everybody likes to discuss. But what about the good days? Does Joe remember every detail about a good day? Perhaps. He may not though because people focus on the bad, the bad gives greater sympathy from others, the good may cause jealousy because it didn't happen to them.

It may be interesting to know the one little thing that controls 90% of our actions and our reactions. Ego. One should be more clear on the term, it is to say that egotism is the culprit at work here. If Joe was to embrace the theories of Freud, the ego is categorized into three separate parts: id, ego and super-ego.

The id is the primal, instinctual part of Joe's psyche that has been present from the moment his brain entered a conscious state to the inevitable end of his being. It is the driving force behind the need for instant gratification, the part that acts purely on impulse. It is a selfish id therefore, from here on we shall call it Sid. As newborn, Joe knew absolutely nothing. There were not enough experiences or intelligence to learn from as of yet but he instinctually understood any discomfort - hunger, thirst, crappy nappy, tired, awake, colic, hiccups - as things that needed to be taken care of right away, so he cried. When he got what he needed, he reverted back to a state of comfort.

Later in Joe's life, Sid is still urging him towards the immediate fulfillment based on impulses. In males, it must push much harder for if Joe sees a naked woman the sudden impulse is to have sex with her. The primal part of him is telling his body that is there is a signal for reproduction and he better get on it - so to speak.

Joe also experiences Sid when he sees something he wants and he may feel an impulse to take it. The development of our character, thankfully, has learned to control that urge to some extent, that's why Joe would unconsciously pick it up or touch it. He would be acting on Sid and controlling it at the same time. Unfortunately, Sid is a far greater force in many people and they have not the will to tone him down.

The opposite end of Sid is the super-ego. Its function is to be the parent to the Sid child and curb his desire for instant gratification. Essentially, the Jiminy Cricket to Pinocchio. The super-ego has to be nourished and influenced over time through guidance and experience, it has to learn and develop the sense of right and wrong. But it can be cruel for that part of Joe wants him to be perfect and will tell him he is too fat or too skinny, or he doesn't look just right. It manages the guilt as well and will make him feel bad for eating that extra piece of cake or indulge in that extra marital affair should the opportunity arise.

The ego part is the mediator between Sid and super-ego it uses common sense. It measures reality and attempts to satisfy the other two to maintain balance with Joe's psyche. The ego must suppress the impulses of Sid while satisfying the super-ego's particular needs for perfection. Since Sid's demands tend to ignore reality and morals, the super-ego works for or against self-expectation, the ego uses direct outside influence to lessen the tensions between the two to forge a more well-rounded individual personality.

Now Joe should be able to watch news stories about theft, rape or murder and understand how fragile the connections of the ego can be. One faulty wire in either direction can cause a serious lack of judgement in social normalcy, or detrimental opinions of self-worth. Sid can overpower if there has been a serious lack of proper outside stimuli or the super-ego can take control with an insufficient amount of positive reinforcement. This brings Joe to a greater understanding of what it is to be human. A deeper connection is being formed and Joe can see parts of himself in everybody else. With this knowledge, he would begin to seek out those whose eyes are as opened as his and his thirst for knowledge will grow.

Joe will experience a longing for community. He will want to live in a world where people look out for one another. Where the needs of the many out way the needs of the few. When everyone is working for the benefit of all, no one is going without. Positive influence nurtures the ego and greater harmony is achieved within the psyche causing less stress and anxiety, less need to fulfill immediate desires, a sense of personal worth that does not need to strive to please the opinions of somebody else.

Joe wants euphoric conditions where outside stimuli is not found in artificial influences such as drugs, alcohol or crime. A place where there are no effects of stress due to deadlines and schedules. Such perceptions were not how things were meant to be, it's just how things developed.

Give A Sh!t

NOTICE

TEMPORARILY OUT OF SERVICE

How Joe becomes a better person at this point lies within how much he cares and what about. Time has passed, he has had opportunity to adjust to his jobless lifestyle and he knows he will have to find some sort of income before his benefits run out, but not right now. He entertains a desire to change his career, perhaps focus on something more creative and intuitive with less hours and less stress.

He has researched this topic of what true freedom means and found terms like 'freeman of the land', and 'strawman', and wondered if there was any true stock in them. To be a real free man of the land sounds euphoric, the potential for Eden on Earth unbound by the constraints of the modern world. But that leads to its own problems like traveling, self-sufficiency, virtually not having a means of proving Joe is who he says he is. There's so much more to take into consideration, not an impossibility by any means but Joe would have to learn how to power his own house, grow, kill and process his own food, do his own maintenance on everything he owns. He would still need an income if he wants to continue satellite tv, internet, cell phone and other modern luxuries of his age. And he would have to do it on a chunk of land the government doesn't own should he prove he doesn't need to pay taxes on it.

How much does Joe care and what about... Does he care enough to chase after the system to prove he has every right to live and be free without the complications of documents and courts? Knowing exactly what to say at the moment he gets a ticket for no license or insurance? Having the endless research into the proper documents and explain in the courtroom that he is not JOE but the individual representing the JOE entity? At some point, Joe is going to ask himself, what is going to make my life easier? Definitely not by red flagging the JOE entity and drawing undo attention to himself.

Getting out of the system is not a simple matter as Joe saying, "I'm out!" and just like that, no more worries. It takes time and millions more people to come to the same conclusion and universally agree to stand up and make that kind of change. A shift like that is only just beginning to sprout and it needs the right encouragement and fertilizer if it is going to develop a strong enough root system to support the whole tree. That is what things need to be, a tree. Several individuals (branches) supported from a community (trunk) supported by functional network (roots) that nourishes the whole.

After a few weeks of his new lifestyle, Joe started stressing about what he was going to do. When he started to learn about the backwards system he lives in, he got angry and stressed about that. Then he started thinking about how he was going to get out of the system, the problems he would have to face if he successfully separated Joe from JOE - meaning rescinding his social insurance number, unregistering his birth certificate and compiling all of the necessary documents he would need to have quick access to to prove the system cannot lawfully touch him. That stressed him out too.

Where instead should he put that energy? It would be much better used discovering what he will do next over brooding about what already happened. Sh!t happens, deal with it Joe and move on.

It seems no matter his choice of action, the reaction was stress. Stress is a silent killer. It wears down Joe's emotions, his physical being and his mind. It causes all sorts of afflictions he can live better without. He will stress about being stressed, feel guilty about feeling guilty, feel bad about feeling bad. That's how it works though, harsh emotions compounding on top of each other and cycling round and round because he cares too much about the crap. Joe needs to understand there are things he cannot change, like getting laid off, and no amount of stress or worry before or after being laid off would change the fact that he got laid off. It was inevitable so why should he put forth so much time and energy into the whole affair? Worrying about if it was going to happen, stressing after it happened, neither changed the outcome of the event. Stress a little, stress a lot, does not matter, it still happened.

The media told Joe he needed a better job, a better truck, a better house the newest phone on the market. Having such things is the mark of a successful person living a successful life, so says media. Joe finally saw through all that crap. Striving for those things coated his entire being with the stress of constantly working for it all and trying to pay it all off. What happens five years after Joe finally gets that new truck paid for? It's no longer new, the warranties have run out and Sid is screaming at him to get a new one because Bill just did and he's plastered pictures of it all over Facebook. The id part of egotism is never satisfied, ever. Once Joe has busted his ass to get where it told him to be, Sid would have nothing to do and that will not do at all so it creates another thing for Joe to want, or convince him he needs. *Striving but never arriving*, as noted more than once by Dr. Wayne Dyer.

Wayne's concept was to prove that Joe's egotism would convince him that he needed more and better things or accomplishments in his life to reach happiness and fulfillment. That he has to constantly prove himself to others to show his quality and his worth and for it to mean anything. Such a belief only feeds Sid, where the ego can no longer attempt to balance and Joe is left constantly striving to satiate it but never arriving to a point where Sid stops asking. Joe's higher self, his spirit, never asks such things of him. It never asks him to sacrifice and struggle, never makes him believe he is a failure because he not striving for something more.

If Joe cared more to listen to his higher spirit, he would find a greater appreciation for himself. Not a self that becomes lazy and lethargic with bliss, without purpose or sense of accomplishment, but rather a simple lack of need to prove anything to anyone else. What would Joe then do with his life? He would find himself more creative and more productive, ready to go head strong into the next project he is intuitively drawn towards. He would know everything is provided for him, just by following his instincts and the signs presented to him, he would be shown where to go to get what he needs.

Simply put, the moment Joe releases any concerns about success, how others see his worth and what he needs to do next to be happy he sheds the weight from his shoulders and success comes to him. As for happiness? Dr. Dyer put it best, there is no way to happiness, happiness is the way.

Though there is another side to such a concept, as introduced by Mark Manson in his book, *The Subtle Art of Not Giving a F*ck*. Mr. Manson agrees to the not trying principle and success will come and adds that Joe obsesses over being happier and healthier and better to the point he is convinced such goals are the be all and end all of the happy trail to enlightenment. But spiritual bliss comes at a paradoxical price. The only way to achieve oneness and be more complete with himself, Joe needs to initiate a mantra he will recite every day which actually affirms that which he lacks. If Joe wants to draw success into his life, his mantra will have to acknowledge the fact that he currently has no success. Joe's egotism must be sporting a heavy migraine by this point. To not be a loser, Joe has to admit he is a loser... Counterproductive.

Such changes in Joe's life are not easy to facilitate by himself. What he will look for now are like minds. He will search for books and audio media that will teach him how to achieve an inner calm and a more grounded touch with his sensibilities. He may find the works of Dr. Wayne Dyer, Doreen Virtue, The Tao Te Ching or even the Bible for spiritual reference. None of these are bad things and when put into a deeper perspective with the thoughts of Mark Manson, everything comes into balance.

By caring about the right things in life.

What Joe needs is a sense of community. This is the beginning of a longing for connection, to be reunited with the whole from which he has been separated since his induction into the system. Joe has figured out everybody feels the same way, everybody feels disconnected and that is why they strive so hard to fit in, perhaps they are just misguided as to where they are supposed to fit in. Society today has its own plethora of social classifications: white collar, blue collar, elite, corporate kings, working class, poor, black, white,

Latino, native, Muslim, Christian, Catholic, nerd, jock, emo, princess, king, queen, duke, earl... Joe wouldn't think finding someplace to fit in would be so difficult with so many options.

But it is difficult. Largely due to none of these classifications or groups are the right ones. Meaning, none of them provide true fulfillment and enrichment. They don't nurture Joe's spirit or challenge his soul or feed his intellect. All of the current options are kindred to Manson's paradoxical system, they try to unite groups based on what keeps them separate.

Mind blown.

The community Joe seeks is one where there is no separation based on race, religion, social standing, income or title. Just a bunch of people doing what needs to be done to survive and live happily ever after. The pursuit of career still exists for the community still needs carpenters, plumbers, healers, herbalists and gardeners, tailors and spiritual guides, the benefit is not a higher rate of pay but trade and equal support. The healer cures the carpenter of his explosive diarrhea so the carpenter helps construct the doctor's new greenhouse. The doctor does not know much about gardening so the gardener helps him get set up and started and the doctor mends the gardener's son's recently broken arm. A constant cycle of each providing for another and no one is left without. True equality and support because people choose to care about the welfare of people instead of their own position in the hierarchy.

But Joe understands this system does not yet exist because not enough people are open to it. Such a way of life couldn't be possible because it's too euphoric, too unnatural, too unbelievable, too - too good to be true.

That's what they choose to believe.

Holy Sh!t

Joe has thought about death. Life continues without his interference and he knows this because after he leaves this world, he will no longer be around to try to control anything that happens anywhere and the world will still get along. After a while, he has really come to figure a lot of stuff out. He has come to realize that life is much easier when he does not stress about everything he cannot change.

And in that moment, he found peace.

Though he would have to admit it was a difficult path to tread, mostly uphill and full of rocks and thorny branches of frustration but the top boasted a serene view where there was nothing to do but live and breathe and go where the wind would take him. The world's problems would sort themselves out and if Sid begged him to intervene, well, tough toodles he thought.

People will see Joe's perspective as odd but so what? That is also not his concern. His outlook will draw to him people who see things as he does and he may be surprised at how big that number really is. Everybody has that side within them, most simply choose to ignore it because they have a different crowd they want to fit into at the moment. It is not Joe's place to sway them for everyone learns who they are in their own way and at their own pace. That's what the universe has laid out for them just as what it had laid out for Joe. For others, the first glimmer of light may start with relating to a quote that seems to have an accord more than others. Or an action or truly great deed done by someone that pulls a little harder on the ole heart strings. Mankind has been forged to be drawn to sacrifice and heroics from the start. Did Christ not sacrifice himself for the sins of man and is mankind not still moved by it? Are not the stories of true heroes passed on from generation to generation? Do we not still find the happily ever after ending to stories more meaningful and satisfying than hopeless tragedy? It is not that mankind has shied away from that which inspires, just that such things have been twisted to play on a society's emotions to convince Joe to dig deeper into his pockets and shell out more cash.

Joe hasn't spent much time in a church either. He has gone a couple of times when a girlfriend talked him into going but he quickly realized it wasn't for him. Apparently, neither was the girlfriend when she realized she couldn't talk him into going again, she told him they were going in different directions and they should see other people.

Holy water under the golden bridge, Joe moved on but not without having deep thoughts as to why committed religion did not suit him. He noticed a pattern similar in all levels of organized parties. The masses, Joe likes to refer to as sheep, are corralled into an area and are told what to believe, how to think and how to behave by the shepherds. Just like the system with all their regulations and laws and media. It is another structure where a person or group of people use fear tactics to coerce the sheep into a behavioral pattern of obedience. In the church's case, they use the fear of God. The sheep are warned that if certain behaviours are not followed then it is eternal damnation for the soul - burning pits and brimstone, occasional jabs in the ribs by a red man with horns and a tail wielding a pitchfork.

With a vision like that how could one not conform? That is the power the church has had over mankind since the discovery of the deity. It was nothing more than an excuse to exercise power and control. Joe seriously doubts that is what God had mind when He first showed himself and probably the reason why He shut the hell up after a while. Joe would too if someone took his word and used it to force another into submission. It's backwards and defeats the purpose of what was trying to be accomplished.

The contrast within the religious sect is even so blatantly outlandish, Joe has to laugh at it for it exemplifies the misuse of power. Every time he sees the Pope in the news and thinks about where he gets to live and the lifestyle he has, he doesn't look like he struggles all that much, or makes sacrifices for the benefit of his sheep. It looks like he is treated like a king, a truly powerful figure able to storm into the queen's chambers and tell her what's what. He is anointed with a large salary, dressed in fine cloth and housed in a cathedral. All very luxurious for being a proclaimed 'man of God'. Joe gets the impression he looks down into the barnyard and says, 'I'm rich and powerful and you're not, too bad for you. It is because I worship better and God has given me the gifts I deserve.'

Look at the churches, 'houses of God' that used to be a simple, one room buildings where good people could go and pray and feel closer to

God. Now, a church is an expensive, ornate, gold laced, monolithic embellishment of a structure that goes way beyond the means of its purpose. Homeless people on the streets and these buildings stand empty for most of the week. Massive sums of money go into them and if there's a little left over, a small soup kitchen gets a new pot.

No, Joe couldn't see himself making a lifestyle out of going to church every Sunday to repent, confess his sins, sin again during the week - which is okay because he'll confess and be forgiven every Sunday - and look poorly on his fellow man because he is not going to church every Sunday. He doesn't need someone else telling him how to think and how to act. He doesn't need another political party exacting power over him. Mankind should not be so hung up on trying to control mankind but it sure finds any excuse to do so. Religion separates people, it gives people an excuse to go to war. 'My god is better than your god' is too playground antics to justify the mass slaughter of a culture. The term 'spirituality' however, gives rise to oneness, a singular belief where it does not matter the name of the god, only that the actions of the believer reflect good intentions. Speak openly, pray silently, shout from the hilltop, but do not force it upon others with declarations that any belief is the one and only truth. Such behaviour inflicts hostility and not good intentions. It takes from people their freedom of choice.

Joe looked up the names of the most known gods in history and noticed a shining singularity: God, Ra, Buddha, Jehovah, Allah, Khuda, Krishna... they possess the same short a sound. As Dr. Wayne Dyer has explained, it is the simplest sound, needing the absolute least amount of effort to make. It is used in meditation to connect with the source and quiet the mind. All of these gods no longer seem all that different now.

Forcing any one belief is not how Christ did it. It's not how truly good souls like Mother Teresa did it. Joe saw the contrast immediately and knew for himself who the false profits were. JC did not preach from a podium and neither did MT, they went out into the world and gave of themselves. They did not demand religious conversion or see anyone as separate or different in any way. They spread love and hope and good will. They asked for nothing in return but faith. And in return God did not shower them in gold and luxuries but instead He gave them a life of happiness, purpose and people who loved them back. They never went for wanting for everything was provided and though they looked to live poorly they were far richer than the Pope will ever be.

But Joe admits that it is a huge change in

lifestyle to go from taking to giving in the same manner as those two angels on earth. Current life choices and the system hinder such devotion to others on a full time scale. Joe, his workmates, his friends, his family are all too emotionally committed to the hardships of making ends meet for their own lives. How does anyone make time to selflessly accommodate the needs of complete strangers? One act of random kindness at a time.

It spreads. It's contagious like a disease that makes everyone alive and healthy. It can become an addiction, the gratification of making someone else's life a bit easier. It tends to make people smile. In a time when people want gratification, acceptance and to be remembered for who they are and what they do, nothing accomplishes that better than showing somebody a random act of kindness. That person will remember, and talk about it, not because Joe has sacrificed hours and hours to get that promotion and raise, not because he saved up some money and bought a great house and a great truck and certainly not in the same manner as if he accumulated a few million dollars and owned three houses, five cars, a motorhome, a jet ski and a trophy wife with large breasts and a monster poodle shaved to look like a balloon animal. Joe noticed most rich people are seen as an upper shelf bunch, high society brand of folk who are generally more envied than related to. No, no, not Joe. He will be remembered because he held the door for the single mother with two kids and a stroller trying to do her grocery shopping, or he paid for a complete stranger's coffee in the Tim Horton's drive through. Because he made somebody smile.

A more meaningful religious experience is then found in kindness, sharing, self-sacrifice and understanding and not in how well Joe prays or repents. There were two tablets forged with ten simple commandments that made up all of the rules mankind ever needed. God believed it, why can't mankind? It's a simple choice of exercising right over wrong. Yes, it really is that simple.

One act of random kindness. Then another, and another and soon everyone is participating in the pay it forward system and everyone has their needs met. Joe learns to give and not steal. He doesn't feel the need to get caught up in the drama of other people's lives because it's all superficial reactions of weaker psyches longing for attention.

It is in the advent of reality tv where Joe once misplaced his sense of community, his careless providing of improper concern over trivial matters. Being emotionally involved in the lives of others is always a good investment but not at every detail of those lives. Whether or not they win over their enemies or alliances for a cash prize or fleeting chance at a whimsical, fairy tale marriage through subterfuge is an extreme amount of effort best placed elsewhere. The concern over such matters makes no improvement on Joe's life, he will only feel anguish or frustration when his chosen character does not comply or makes the wrong decision or loses altogether. There will be only a brief moment of glory should that character reign as champion by overcoming all other obstacles before Joe promptly forgets the importance of said character when the next episode or series begins.

When Joe indulges in such behaviour, it spills over into the real world and he desires the same gratification from others, forsaking his spiritually good intentions. It becomes a pattern, an obsession, a never ending struggle for the next fix from the next person and Joe loses sight of his own goals to become a better person. Instead, he must let go. Give all of that unnecessary energy to the universe and find his own peace. Let go of all of the things that would cause him turmoil and stress and anxiety and let the universe sort it out. As Dr. Wayne Dyer put it, let go and let be.

No Sh!t

NOTICE

HELP KEEP THIS PLACE CLEAN

The world has horrible events taking place at every moment, events that can be changed by making a different choice. Joe can make a difference in the world by not acting on the evil against another. Forsaking Sid to follow the more community-minded way, to follow the spirit.

He has tried to partake in conversation about his new thinking but he is generally met with strange glances and conflicting opinions from others and he is okay with that because some others are not yet open to the reality that there is another way of doing things. This way of life is how it has been done for centuries and that is just how things are. Joe understands now because he has been there, he thought the same way once. He knows also that his mind was changed, just like anybody's mind can be changed, through an event in his life that brought him face to face with the reality and 'how it is' was slapped across his face like a iron gauntlet. That is how it must be with others, they must face their own realities in their own way.

People have come and gone in his life and more people will continue to come and go. These are experiences Joe must accept to get him where he is supposed to be. Each experience brings with it a new lesson and when Joe has learned that lesson, the experience is done and a new one comes into his life. Only when was open to this reality was he able to see it for what it is.

Joe can see it so plainly, so easily and so clearly how a better life can be achieved if enough people want it. The path to a life of no sh!t lies in perception. Mankind must realize, with brutal impact, the devastation this way of life has done to ourselves and to our planet. To maim and kill is done for sport and pleasure with no impact on the conscience or the soul. The weight of taking a life has no bearing at all, to destroy a complete living being composed of thoughts, hopes, inspirations, a soul connected to universal knowledge snuffed out to satisfy another's end game. Proof to Joe that man cannot control himself, cannot rule himself or govern himself.

Yet.

There is a better way. It cannot be denied because it can't be seen or touched. It can be felt, it can be dreamed and brought to fruition through will. There are no gains from entitling a person to believe that failure does not exist and there are little to no consequences to certain actions. Wrong is wrong. Failing is natural and not a devastating wound that leaves a scar on the psyche. These are learning tools to teach Joe the balance and appreciation of the order of things. They happen so he will become more capable and better equipped to conduct himself and make good decisions. People just aren't making good decisions anymore. Decisions are made mostly on personal gain or self-promotion not for the benefit of all as God may have originally intended.

What is Joe to know of God's intentions though? He has been told man was created in His image and man has always taken the literal definition. Or the backwards one - God looks like a man, he is typically portrayed as elderly white chap (no offense Mr. Freeman) with long flowing white hair and beard dressed in a simple white robe; corporeal, having a body and physical form. This is the image Joe assumed man was created from and that's why he looks as he does. But Joe has learned things, he has knowledge he did not have before.

The notion of His image is now a naiveté and he thinks the true image was the mind and spirit, not the body, not the corporeal.

Holy eureka does that lift veils to fresh understanding! Darwin can still be right - on the physical reality - and spiritual belief can also be right - on the spiritual reality. The crappy differences are now mingled to a singular perception that fills the gaps to the mystery of man's evolution. Nature and environment does affect the evolutionary change in biology, life could have begun from planetary alignments causing the right conditions for a single celled organism to develop into the myriad of complex creatures that roam the Earth. Perhaps God did not create Adam from a pile of dirt and Eve from Adam's rib but instead, allowed an evolutionary leap from monkey to man and bestowed upon him a conscience - a mind and spirit, the image of God. The concept may not be right but it answers some questions, like where Neanderthal man and the like fit into the picture, how mankind reproduced from Adam and Eve's three sons, or how it continued from Noah's children. Does that not add some levity to current affairs where previously taboo topics such as homosexuality and incest now have to be believed as the only means of mankind's continued existence at the beginning and after the flood.

Truly, it doesn't matter if the concept is right or wrong, none now live today to say things happened either way and Joe figures if it's that important, he can ask when he arrives in the afterlife. What should matter is what we know to be right and wrong. Not through literal interpretations or speculations of past events recorded even before man's creation that must be taken on faith as absolute. The physical body Joe was born into has separated him from the image and his connection to the spirit and the purpose of his life just may be to rebuild that connection. The story unfolds with its own theme: man sins, learns, seeks forgiveness, betters himself. It is the basic structure of character development told in nearly every story. Thus, by the end of the story, the bond with the spirit grows stronger as the character overcomes the obstacles and learns to be a better person. Again and again the story plays out but with less people seeking forgiveness and betterment of self. The obstacles are being removed from them so they don't have to overcome anything and failure is not experienced. The diabolical Sid is now entitled to do as it pleases and would have to convince Joe that to better himself, do things differently next time so he doesn't get caught.

Joe studies the structure of what makes a story acceptable and successful, a structure that has never changed. For a story to work there must be a believable character who is removed from a normal existence, put on a quest, forced to face challenges and emerge triumphantly having a new outlook and understanding on things. He sees the story of mankind and it is still unfinished having begun as normal, gave in to the temptation of sin and have been facing challenges and obstacles ever since. Slowly, conditions have created opportunities for the characters to reach a critical choice in their journey - to decide right or wrong - and either continue on the same path, waiting for another condition or they leap forward, reaching a climax to use the newfound knowledge to clear the last obstacles, realize the change in perception and commit to it. Happily ever after.

The story only truly ends when the connection with the spirit is achieved and there is nothing left for it to learn on earth. The soul is returned to the universe, the source of it all and Joe knows not what happens after. His story is not done yet either. He has his own story as every person has their own and they are merely sub-stories to the whole of mankind and there are no spoilers to that ending. It will unfold as it must, each person like Joe seeking others who have the vision and wish to share, to improve and to seek community. Yes, there is frustration at the way things are, at the defenselessness of not being able to change it all right now, of knowing how better things can be if only... Ah, if only... if only it were all that simple mankind would be there already, not killing, not destroying, not controlling, not forcing, not striving.

Just being and letting things just be.

The true great secrets of the universe hiding in plain sight yet out of reach because Sid wants Joe to believe it is far more complex than that, man's reason for being. There is more, there has to more to it for is not man special? Is he not God's favourite? Who is to say, Joe thinks. In all the galaxies, in all the universes - that man has not yet explored - to believe man is alone is its own selfish naiveté. Can planetary alignments creating the perfect conditions have not occurred somewhere else? Could God have not sparked another image of Himself somewhere else believing He could do better, or already has done worse? After all, if it is in man's nature to fail and learn, why not Him for after whose image man was created? In story, nothing happens without a reason, if man is not privy to that reason or he does not understand it, it does not make it wrong or unfair or unjust. It just means the reason remains unknown.

I Sh!t You Not

I could be one those guys who go on and on about how I was one of those people who was never understood, who felt about things differently, saw things differently, had a different thought process but I confess, what's the point? It doesn't make me special or all that different really. Lots of people are just like me, they sees things as I do and seek to share and find others just like them.

Frankly, I am beyond wanting to put in the energy it takes to be concerned about how others view who I am and try living up to that ideal. There are just too many. Everyone has a different opinion about who I am supposed to be, what I am supposed to do, how I am supposed to do it. I don't care about that anymore. I care as much about having peace and order in the universe as I do in my own house - which is a lot and why I am always frustrated when I can't seem to figure out how to achieve it.

The thoughts I have amassed here are not for everybody, that much is clear for not everybody is alike. My perceptions are as different from a complete stranger as they are from my own brother. He walks his path as I walk mine. Physically, we may share the same DNA, but spiritually, our souls have travelled different paths through different walks of life at different times. Parentage makes us related physically on this earth, the source makes us related off of it. That's my belief, probably not his.

My ideas on things were accumulated over time from experience, reading, watching, listening and putting two and two together but something had to have been there from the start to create the wanting to know. I believe this because I see so many who seem blind to the experience. They follow the routines and rituals of work, pay bills, sleep, work, all without question. This is how it is, this is what you need to do. People tell me this. I have to learn one thing that will get me one good paying job that I must remain at my entire life, retire only when I am too old to enjoy what's left - provided I can afford to retire at all. I must pay the bills the system forces upon me and if there is any money left over from the vultures, I may be permitted do something for myself.

Sorry, I can't do it. Which is the cause of much of the frustration with my wife as she cannot convince me that's the way it's supposed to be. She bought into the system whole heartedly, there is no other way to do it. I love her to death but I know on that issue, we will never see eye to eye. That and she knows sometimes I put two and two together and get five, or three...

I have been keeping most of my thoughts and perspectives to myself and I have noticed that my ability to interact in much conversation has lessened over the last little while. I am quieter, choosing to listen more than speak because I know if I speak I am expressing opinions and notions that most people are either not accustomed to, don't agree with or aren't ready to hear. That's not to say the only thing I can talk about are my opinions and I only want to ram them down everybody's throat, I just find myself unable to relate with the issues and turmoils everybody else is going through. I have found a greater peace. People like to talk about themselves, especially their drama, and many people ask other people questions merely as a springboard to talk about themselves some more. I don't always remember the details of conversations but I do note the patterns that are similar from person to person. I don't know why I pay attention to such little details about human interaction but I can't shut it off.

Carrying on conversations where I am made to believe everybody and their life is more important is not interesting conversation. I don't like to talk about myself and my life much or use the word 'I' but this entire chapter is all about me and I use 'I' a lot in it. My apologies but you will have to get used to it or skip to the next chapter but I feel I must indulge in letting the readers of this book have some insight as to where this information comes from. I'm not cynical and I don't hate people, I should point that out. People are equal across the board and should not try to see themselves as better by talking about themselves and relating their experience as being better, more special, more tragic or more difficult than someone else. Drama doesn't interest me. No one's life has ever been improved by focusing on the drama they put themselves through. Drama to me is an extremely weak attempt to extort attention from others. It shows a personality that cannot sustain itself and must use emotional pity for support. Unfortunately, this the theme of all reality shows so you can deduce how many of those I watch. How can anybody think so little of themselves they would subject their character to such public belittlement? Sid has your answer. Sid wants attention and is always the first to remind you that you are not good enough.

It's just who I am. Not anybody special, just a guy who has some thoughts that plagued me until I was inspired to write them down. I am not a professional in anything. I have not been fully educated in any single field. I don't even have a high school diploma. I know in today's conventions that makes me someone without the knowledge and experience to write about anything or try to prove I know anything about anything. I didn't read the bible from cover to cover, nor did I read up on everything there is to know about political sciences to tell anyone how the government works. I have not made it as far as I have because of a diploma, a PhD, or a certificate. I made it because I proved I knew something about something and I can use it to help. It hasn't made me rich and successful and there are still months where there isn't much left over but where I am in life is not determined by what everybody else sees as successful.

Neither am I a poor individual. I have not struggled to obtain things or support my family until the oilfield shut down in Alberta and I had to rely on employment insurance benefits to get by. I tried looking for another job but then my daughter exploded her femur in a horse accident and I became an at home dad to look after her. But I am a writer and I turned to what I know to try to make ends meet while I can't go to work and while my daughter is learning to walk again. I have time to follow a passion, my daughter and I have strengthened our relationship, all after I spent months wondering how I was going to finish that trilogy I have been working on for years and why I wasn't as close to my daughter as I wanted to be. Put a thought out there and the universe takes care of things - though not always in the ways we hope or expect.

While others will dismiss my lack of credentials to write about a topic, or any topic, I honestly don't see as a concern. Especially about the topic of this book. Do I have to be a psychiatrist or theologian to rant about my perspectives and ideas on life? Do I have to prove to be better than someone else to justify what I write? These are my opinions that I share, founded and built from experience and noticing what is going on; feelings, patterns and gut instinct and an unyielding desire to get it out there. Some things have to be acted upon regardless of the outcome because the universe is trying to tell you something. I may be shunned as an outcast later, I may be dismissed as a quack and lose all association with friends and family because I couldn't keep my thoughts to myself. I may be shot or incarcerated because I believe that if I ever met the queen face to face, I would not show her any more respect as a human being than any other human being - well maybe sympathy from the absurd amount of pressure she would have to endure from having her title. That's gotta be rough!

Because that's who I am. She is a queen because of a title established and given to her by man's doings just as the prime minister is a prime minister because mankind developed a means to exercise power over others. To me, they are titles and nothing more. These people are just people, having no special powers bestowed upon them to smash the will of everybody else. These titles were not given to them by God, nor do I believe God would even condone the idea. These are man-made contrivances and cannot have power over the God-given freedoms of man himself. These powers we have established over time do more to harm towards how we should view each other than anything that has ever existed. They strive to separate and create weakness because weak and unintelligent is easier to control. God gave us ten commandments and honestly, if we had the will to exercise good will towards men, why would we need anything else?

Sin and temptation, you slippery snake. Sin and temptation.

So if I was to ever confront the queen and I do not bow or say 'your majesty' and she gets offended and has me publicly beheaded for treason, then I do so willingly and freely for she has proven I was right about how the system works to control the people. After I'm dead I will be that much closer to the answers I seek and the world will still turn without me. If there is nothing to go to in the afterlife, well I won't know to give a shit anyway.

Sh!ts & Giggles

NOTICE

RESPIRATORS REQUIRED IN THIS AREA

Life was not created to be taken so seriously. We were designed to love and laugh and learn from our mistakes. Every day to think, 'I have to do this', 'I have to do that' is a mantra for destruction and in no way a description to live a life successfully. A truly successful life on Earth is not measured in the accumulation of money and stuff, but in the accumulation of laugh lines and friends.

I enjoy the outdoors and try to get outside as often as possible, all year round. I will stay in a hunting camp or my preferred method, a plastic shelter between two trees and just enjoy my surroundings. It never ceases to amaze me how much time a person can burn through just sitting and staring into a fire. No pressure, nothing gnawing at me to complete or start; just me, the fire, the trees and maybe a friend or two. This is the type of activity everybody needs to partake in on a regular basis to be reminded of what serenity feels like. It can become an addiction. Find your thing that brings you to that completely peaceful state of mind and make time to do it. Lie in your yard or on your deck and watch the clouds or the stars. Watch for satellites and shooting stars and be taken aback how your mind places everyday problems and worries on the back burner.

Many different people will form different opinions about this book and I am not going to stress about it. It's just information I wanted to share and anybody is free to think I'm a certifiable whacko or just weird, strange, different or perhaps enlightened, insightful, observant, or intelligent. The stress or anguish any negative comments forwarded to me about my opinion come from people no less intelligent nor more intelligent than I. They are opinions offered and if I let them get to me, I concede to defeat and add to my problems. That is not conducive to a better state of mind and I view that such people who need to strive so hard to put others down are themselves, not in a good state of mind to offer advice on how to improve. I welcome any comments, no matter how harsh, for that is how I can learn where my opinions fit into the grand scheme of things, whether I am on the right track to figuring things out. Sharing opinions is a great way for anybody to learn and develop a better, more constructive grasp on their reality.

The idea is not to shun this work for its contradictory nature but have it raise questions, to see if it feels right, to find the truth. If it insights any aspirations to be better and treat people better, I know I am doing something good in the world. If it inspires communication and discussion, I know I am helping to shift perceptions and people are opening up to new possibilities. If it just simply irritates the crap out of everybody and causes them to fire insults and negative banter, then I know I am he who needs to shift my perceptions and be open to any possibilities. Either way, I am learning while I hope to educate and inspire, I am finding hope while I reach out to like minds and I try to giggle a bit more each day instead of stewing over how much of an asshole somebody else may be. I am perceived as much of an ass for the action for it does not improve my standing as a person of inspiration or enlightenment.

Determine who you are and who you want to be as a person. There is a lot of shit in the world and there are an insurmountable more reasons to giggle. Laugh at yourself in an embarrassing situation, how else are you going to deal with it? Get mad? Run and hide? Shit happens, laugh and move on. It's not always easy but it works. You can strive to be a person who towers above others and claim to be better, richer, or smarter but know you do so not for the respect and appreciation of your fellow humans but for their submission to the power you want over them. Rich, powerful people are simply envied, nothing more.

Or, you can be a person who inspires. Someone who does not strive to better themselves but to better the world - though not by striving but through simple acts of random kindness. By showing others how to live better and freer without hate or anger towards others. When you remember different famous people, what do you remember about them and what do you feel when you remember them? People like Mandala, Mother Theresa, Terry Fox or the Dalai Lama; or perhaps people like, Trump, Oprah, the Kardashians... who you inspire to be like says much about the type of person you are.

Laugh more. Inspire to laugh more. Find a peaceful place and visit it often. Stress cannot find you there, worry melts from your shoulders and serenity fills every part of your being.

And for God's sake, stop giving a shit about every little thing!

More

Stay tuned for the follow up title

Out Of The Crapper

More information about the ideas found in this book can be found at www.harebrain.ca

www.ingramcontent.com/pod-product-compliance
Lightning Source LLC
LaVergne TN
LVHW012046070526
838201LV00079B/3646